The Shape of Rainbows

Dedicated to all my fantastic family and friends – they know who they are! – N.Z.

To Granny Pat, thank you for encouraging me to draw and come up with stories. – W.H.

Text copyright © Neal Zetter 2024
Illustrations copyright © Will Hughes 2024

First published in Great Britain in 2024 by
Otter-Barry Books, Little Orchard, Burley Gate,
Herefordshire, HR1 3QS
www.otterbarrybooks.com

A catalogue record for this book is available
from the British Library

Designed by Arianna Osti

ISBN 978-1-915659-16-3

Illustrated with line drawings
Printed in Great Britain

1 3 5 7 9 8 6 4 2

The Shape of Rainbows

Poems by Neal Zetter

Illustrated by
Will Hughes

Otter-Barry BOOKS

Contents

Part-Time Superhero

When done with my poems and finished with
   rhymes
I turn to a favourite pastime of mine
In body-tight costume I'm wiping out crime
I'm a part-time superhero

I stop concentrating on publishing books
Instead I climb buildings with grappling hooks
And scour the city for gangsters and crooks
I'm a part-time superhero

Diverting attention from poetry texts
I'm strengthening muscles, displaying them pecs
Now mighty enough to floor any T-Rex
I'm a part-time superhero

I pack both my pen and my pencil away
Then switch my attention to saving the day
If filling out tax forms I frequently say
I'm a part-time superhero

Each morning creating inspiring verse
Each evening defending the whole universe
From four-headed aliens, monsters and worse
I'm a part-time superhero

Most authors I know think me totally nuts
But many applaud me for courage and guts
With two jobs I'll never be stuck in a rut
I'm a part-time superhero

So gaze into space and you'll catch me in flight
Or down on the ground finding villains to fight
Remember, I'm not just a person who writes...

I'm a part-time superhero

Peanut Butter Nutter

I'm a peanut butter nutter
I'm a peanut butter fan
If I was a superhero
I'd be Peanut Butter Man

Love it smooth and love it crunchy
Mixed together's tasty too
For my breakfast or my lunchy
It's the food I choose to chew

I'm not bothered if you see me
Stick a finger in the jar
Don't want marmalade or honey
It's my favourite by far

Beigey brown and sometimes salty
Perfect snack that's protein-packed
Such a source of satisfaction
Cures a hunger pang attack

Yummy on a scoop of ice cream
Scrumptious sandwiched with some jam
Need a peanut butter champion?
Then remember who I am

I'm a peanut butter nutter
Nothing's better on my bread
There's no other name I utter
When I'm asked to pick a spread

One

One is single
On its own
One is separate
All alone
Solo
'Un' in French
In Spanish, 'uno'.

One has no partner
One has no pair
One needs no sofa
Only a chair
One is good at solitaire.

One may be me
One may be you
But one is definitely not two
One might feel isolated
Possibly lonely or frustrated.

One next to one reads as eleven
$1 + 1 + 1 + 1 + 1 + 1 + 1 = 7$
One stands proud as a number
Shaped like a dead straight cucumber.

One is not even
One is odd
One is a sole pea in a pod
One is detached
One is unique
One may be labelled a bit of a freak.

One doesn't ride a tandem
One rides a bike
One is independent and does what it likes
One is high performing, top of the charts
You are my special one who's captured my heart.

One is sometimes sad
One is frequently fun
So don't take it away
Because then...
There'll be none.

Brother Versus Sister

He said YES
She said NO
He said TO
She said FRO
He said WEAK
She said STRONG
He said RIGHT
She said WRONG

He said DO
She said DON'T
He said WILL
She said WON'T
He said HORSE
She said COW
He said ZAP!
She said POW!

He said YOUNG
She said OLD
He said HOT
She said COLD
He said A
She said B
He said SHE
She said HE

He said DOG
She said CAT
He said THIN
She said FAT
He said FLIP
She said FLOP
Till Mum said
STOP! STOP! STOP!

Police Car

Nee-nee, nah-nah
Nee-nee, nah-nah
Nee-nee, nah-nah
I'm a police car

Siren screeching, flashing light
Twisting, turning through the night
Helping to uphold the law
Hear my engine rip and roar

Nee-nee, nah-nah
Nee-nee, nah-nah
Nee-nee, nah-nah
I'm a police car

If a crook commits a crime
I'm there in the nick of time
Never ever call me 'slow'
Grab my steering wheel and GO!

Nee-nee, nah-nah
Nee-nee, nah-nah
Nee-nee, nah-nah
I'm a police car

Swerving, curving round the bend
Robbers, thieves to apprehend
Other traffic's left for dead
While I'm racing on ahead

Nee-nee, nah-nah
Nee-nee, nah-nah
Nee-nee, nah-nah
I'm a police car

Find me in the fastest lane
To the rescue yet again
Speed limits are not for me
999! Emergency!

Nee-nee, nah-nah
Nee-nee, nah-nah
Nee-nee, nah-nah
I'm a police car, I'm a police car

I'm a police caaaaaaaaaaaaar!

The Poem Machine

You plug me in,
you flick my switch,
my brain will buzz,
my fingers twitch.
Then words appear
upon my screen…
I am the poem machine!

With language skills
so legendary,
a robot built
for literacy,
the kingpin of
the poetry scene.
I am the poem machine!

I whir and click,
producing rhyme,
my rhythms beat
in perfect time,
prodigious, smart,
quick, clever, keen.
I am the poem machine!

I've lived my life
for years and years,
but never short
of great ideas,
inspiring kids,
adults and teens.
I am the poem machine!

Creating odes,
ballads and rap.
You want free verse?
It's here on tap.
My works are one
long endless stream.
I am the poem machine!

Not bothered if
it's day or night,
I'm born to write
and write and write,
now set to go,
lights flashing green.
I am the poem machine!

I am the poem machine
I am the poem machine
I AM THE POEM MACHINE!

Be

Be a lion not a mouse
Be a castle not a house
Be a banquet not a lunch
Be the pick of every bunch

Be an ocean not a stream
Don't be milk but be the cream
Be a boulder not a stone
Be unique and not a clone

Be a tall tree not a twig
Be gigantic not just big
Be a "YES!" not "no" or "might"
And let your confidence IGNITE!

Two Mums

My two mums are better than one,
double the love,
double the fun.
It's an easy equation, a simple sum.
Two mums are better than one.

Twice the mums to read to me,
twice the mums to cook my tea.
How could you possibly disagree?
Two mums are better than one.

My two mums are a perfect pair,
double the hugs,
double the care.
Though having two mothers is rather rare,
two mums are better than one.

Twice the mums to make the rules
and to pick me up from school.
Mum plus another mum's totally cool.
Two mums are better than one.

My two mums are a super team,
double the laughs,
double ice cream.
Why would I want to change anything?
Two mums are better than one.

Twice the mums to buy me sweets,
twice the mums for birthday treats.
Dads are real fab but mums are so neat.
Two mums are better than one.

Two mums are better than one!

Gravity

An apple fell on Isaac Newton
underneath a tree.
He said, "That hurt my head,
I think I'll call it Gravity!"

Gravity's on top of me,
it keeps me on the ground.
It's in the air, below my feet
and everywhere around.
Without it the human race
would be floating into space.

Gravity will drag you,
Gravity will draw you,
Gravity will pull you,
Gravity will floor you.
It's magnetic, it's a force.
It's invisible of course.

Gravity will stop you drifting
like a big balloon.
There's just a little bit of it
On Mars and on the Moon.
So put lead weights or some rocks
in your pockets, shoes and socks.

Gravity's a magic power
that's better than a glue.
It helps things to bounce up and down –
ask any kangaroo.
Watch it make grasshoppers hop,
cause your underpants to drop.

Gravity will grasp you,
Gravity will fix you,
Gravity will grab you,
Gravity will stick you.
One of Mother Nature's tricks.
Turns your feet to heavy bricks.

An apple fell on Isaac Newton
underneath a tree.
He said, "That hurt my head,
I think I'll call it Gravity!"

Hot Chocolate

Hot chocolate, hot chocolate
Plain or white or milk chocolate
Hot chocolate, hot chocolate
Soothing smooth as silk chocolate
Hot chocolate, hot chocolate
Flake dipped in the top chocolate
Hot chocolate, hot chocolate
Never waste a drop chocolate

Hot chocolate, hot chocolate
Dreamy, creamy, sweet chocolate
Hot chocolate, hot chocolate
Guilty pleasure treat chocolate
Hot chocolate, hot chocolate
Best served in a mug chocolate
Hot chocolate, hot chocolate
Get the hot choc bug chocolate
Hot chocolate, hot chocolate
Hot chocolate's HOT!

...perfectly

Enthusiastically
Energetically
Keenly
Carefully
Patiently
Purposefully
Hopefully
Optimistically
Eagerly
Endlessly
Intently
Intensely
Inventively
Assiduously
Ardently
Determinedly
Discerningly
Diligently
Longingly
Yearningly
Avidly
Actively
Curiously
Continuously
Restlessly

Resolutely
Relentlessly
Studiously
Skilfully
Fervently
Frantically
Breathlessly
Zealously
Worriedly
Anxiously
Desperately
I searched a list of appropriate adverbs
For this poem's title
Until finally finding one that fitted...

Interstellar Mum

My mum is interstellar,
zooming up into the atmosphere.
My mum is interstellar,
soaring high into the stratosphere.

Longing to touch stars that twinkle above her,
tells us of alien worlds to discover,
certainly quite an unusual mother.

My mum is interstellar,
frequently visiting nebulae.
My mum is interstellar,
Venus, Mars, Jupiter, Mercury.

Says Saturn's rings are a truly unique sight,
view her through telescopes round about
     midnight,
leaving the Earth like a bullet of bright light.

My mum is interstellar,
flying away in a big tin can.
My mum is interstellar,
Travel the universe – that's her plan.

Thinks that more regular work would be boring,
much prefers inter-galactic exploring,
blasting off daily with space rocket roaring.

My mum is interstellar,
why don't you take a leaf from her book?
My mum is interstellar,
journey the cosmos – go take a look.

When I grow up I won't be a train driver
or own a car or become a bike rider.
Mum has the best job so I'll sit beside her
because my mum
is...

INTERSTELLAR!

Free Time

Don't want to gossip
Speak, chat, shout
Waste minutes, hours
Hangin' out
Don't want to sleep, snooze
Rest, nap, doze
Hum, whistle, sing, chant
Blow my nose
Don't want to strain hard
At the gym
Dig through the rubbish
Down your bin

Don't want to watch, spy
Glimpse, gaze, view
Jive, foxtrot, waltz, twist
Boogaloo
Don't want to dine, lunch
Snack, eat, drink
Scrub both my feet clean
In your sink
Don't want to argue
Moan, fuss, fight

Cos I just want to
Sit and write

The Shape of Rainbows

Years ago the colours of the rainbow had a massive disagreement.

RED felt he was most popular.
"I am in the blood pumping through every human being and living creature.
None would survive without me."

ORANGE had a different opinion.
"I share my name with the juiciest, healthiest fruit.
I must be the best."

YELLOW thought she was tops.
"You see me in the sun that powers our solar system.
Remove me and everything would cease to exist."

GREEN claimed superiority.
"I paint Mother Nature's trees and plants that cover our amazing planet.
I am life itself."

BLUE stated his importance.
"Earth's magnificent oceans and vast skies would
be nothing without me.
I am everywhere."

INDIGO pressed her case for greatness.
"People admire me for my air of mystery and
beautiful looks.
Precious and rare – that's me."

VIOLET was not to be outdone.
"I have a flower and many girls and women
named after me.
Surely I am number one?"

Unable to agree on this matter,
the colours still argue to this day.
So that's why rainbows are always...
shaped like a frown.

Grab a Book

Open it
Relish it
Ogle it
Cherish it
Hold it
Hug it
Live it
Love it
Cuddle it
Choose it
Hog it
Don't lose it

Let it wow you
Delight you
Entertain you
Excite you
Educate you
Inspire you
Empower you
Fire you

Feel it
Own it
Like it
Loan it
Enjoy it
Explore it
Admire it
Adore it
Befriend it
Believe it
Roll with it
Read it

Go on...
Grab a book

Heart

I'm your heart, your body's pump
Thump, thump
Thump, thump
Thump, thump
Thump, thump

Like a big internal drum
Nestled just above your tum
Working arteries and veins
Powering organs (e.g. brains)

24 hours of the day
When you're young till old and grey
Feeding you from head to toe
Super living dynamo!

I'm your heart, your body's pump
Thump, thump
Thump, thump
Thump, thump
Thump, thump

Feel my rhythm, hear my beat
Regular as marching feet
At your centre, at your core
Shifting blood then shifting more

I'm love's symbol, I'm love's sign
Find me on your Valentine
If I stopped, you'd cease to be
So please take good care of me

I'm your heart, your body's pump
Thump, thump
Thump, thump
Thump, thump
THUMP, THUMP!

I Want to Be a Clown

Floppy feet
Tomato nose
Silly hat
Baggy clothes
Honking hooter
Wobbly scooter
I want to be a clown

Pants on fire
Pale white skin
Lipstick mouth
Stupid grin
Crazy foam blower
Custard pie thrower
I want to be a clown

Make you laugh
Make you scared
Burst balloons
Purple hair
Trouser splitter
Banana skin slipper
I want to be a clown

Funny face
Circus star
Bonkers! Nuts!
Ha! Ha! Ha!
Audience soaker
Practical joker
I want to be a clown

Lexicon of Leisure

Funny filled the air with laughter
Bouncy bounded round the room
Angry shouted in frustration
Bright outshone the doom and gloom

Friendly kissed and hugged her buddies
Sad shed sacks of salty tears
Frightened shrank then shook in terror
Optimistic spread some cheer

Creepy crouched in his dark corner
Shy was too afraid to ask
Lonely lounged in isolation
Clever came top of her class

Till the poet closed his notebook,
put his magic pen away,
saying, "That's enough wordplay for everyone
today!"

Friend

A friend is a buddy, a partner, a pal,
a friend's anywhere, anytime, anyhow.
When you're facing troubles
and worries and woes
a real friend is there and will not let you go.

A friend will fill your lungs with laughter,
a friend will be your sticking plaster,
make you happy ever after.
A safety net,
a sure-fire bet.

A friend is a neighbour, a backer, an aide,
who smooths your rough edges when you're
    worn and frayed.
When loneliness beckons
or hopelessness looms,
their kindness will catapult you to the moon.

A friend will not refuse a mission,
a friend will fuel your optimism,
tough cement that heals division.
Erase the blue
is what they do.

A friend's a companion, a comrade, a chum,
there are other numbers but they're number one.
When days are huge mountains
far too tall to climb,
a friend is the leg-up that's lifting you high.

A friend will not have cause to doubt you,
a friend won't want to live without you
even when disaster clouts you.
Secure as locks,
like solid rocks

A friend is a buddy, a partner, a pal,
a friend's anywhere, anytime, anyhow.

The Poet Tree

In my garden grows a Poet Tree
With gazillions of poems for everybody
Rhythms roll down from its branches to its roots
Do you want inspiration?
Come pick yourself some fruit

Some poems are short
Some poems are long
Some rhyme, some don't
Some sound like a song
Some make you sad
Some make you smile
Some make you...

STOP!

...and think for a while

Some are new
Some you've heard
Some contain made-up magical words

Think of a theme
A title
A topic
You can bet my Poet Tree's got it

Glasses, moustaches, clocks, caterpillars
Cucumbers, odd numbers, chocolate, chinchillas
Daft dogs, fat frogs, kisses, kings, castles
Lamp posts, burnt toast, postmen with parcels

Computers, peashooters, favourite places
Fairies, football, figs, fish, films, funny faces
Comics, electronics, sticky tape, street signs
Big balloons, blue baboons, silver, socks,
    sunshine

In my garden grows a Poet Tree
With gazillions of poems for everybody
Rhythms roll down from its branches to its roots
Do you want inspiration?
Come pick yourself some fruit

'ees

When I see flower 'eds 'looming
I feel extremely sad
Many mini 'easts disappearing
And that surely must 'e 'ad

We human 'eings need them
As do animals, plants and trees
So please, please, please
Save our 'eautiful 'uzzy 'ees

Circle

I'm a circle
I spin round
Like a wheel across the ground
Got no corners
Got no points
Got no edges
Got no joints

Neither triangle
Nor square
You'll find my shape everywhere
On an apple
On a cake
On a saucer
On a plate

I'm a sphere
When in 3D
Draw a letter O – that's me
As a counter
As a clock
As a zero
As a watch

I'm a disc
So I can roll
Like a ball that scores a goal
I'm a penny
I'm a hoop
I'm a planet
I'm a loop

I'm a circle
You can see
I have perfect symmetry
I've no bottom
I've no top
I make endings
With full stops.

Bad Smells

Bad smells
Dirty dogs
Bad smells
Squashed frogs

Bad smells
Pigsties
Bad smells
Dead flies

Bad smells
Rotten eggs
Bad smells
Monster breath

Bad smells
Green slime
Bad smells
Cheese rind

Bad smells
Mud and muck
Bad smells
Yuck, yuck, yuck

Bad smells
Dustbins
Bad smells
Disgusting

BAD SMELLS!

First Day Back

We said our twelve-times table,
mixed decimals and fractions,
made massive sugar crystals
through chemical reactions.
We studied many mini-beasts
and microscopic creatures,
were taught how to respect our friends,
our parents and our teachers.

We climbed on frames in PE,
played boys v girls at football,
at lunchtime I ate pasta,
then ice cream (that was real cool!)
Sir showed us some volcanic rocks,
we spoke a bit of Spanish,
discovered most of Africa,
learnt why the T-Rex vanished.

Next up was comprehension
along with two tough maths tests,
in art we drew self-portraits
but mine looked such a huge mess.
We watched a film on shooting stars,
we visited the library,
did drama in the studio,
completed our day's diary.

Returning home exhausted,
I flopped out on the floor.
Although Year 3 was a great place to be –
I'm already preferring Year 4!

Popcorn!

I like popcorn
Popping in the pan
I like popcorn
I'm its biggest (POP!) fan
I like popcorn
Whether (POP!) salt or sweet
I (POP!) like popcorn
Cos it's neat, neat, (POP!) neat

I like popcorn
Buy (POP!) a mega pack
I like (POP!) popcorn
Such a perfect snack
I like popcorn
Cooked (POP! POP!) but never raw
I like popcorn
Can I (POP!) have some more?

I (POP!) like popcorn
While I watch (POP!) TV
I like popcorn
With a cup of tea (POP!)
I like popcorn
From (POP!) the popcorn shop
I like popcorn
When it pops! Pops! Pops!

POP!

My Many Mes

There's a cheerful me who's happy
There's an upset me who's sad
There's a good me who's an angel
There's a monster me who's bad

There's a me who brims with confidence
There's an unsure me who's shy
There's a me who's ever honest
There's a me who always lies

There's a comic me who's funny
There's a serious me also
There's an early morning miserable me
You wouldn't want to know

There's a keen enthusiastic me
There's a me who's lax and lazy
There is a quiet thoughtful me
There's an angry me who's crazy

There's a me who is so selfish
There's a me who is so kind
There are lost mes I've not seen in years
There are those I've yet to find

And each me's an ingredient
For a special recipe
Cos when all mixed together
They're my personality

Listen

It's the bang of a drum
It's a sweet tune to hum
Popping burst bubblegum
Just listen

It's the news on TV
It's a storm in the sea
Tweeting birds in a tree
Just listen

It's a loud clanging bell
It's a scream, it's a yell
I've a secret to tell
Just listen

It's the bark of a hound
It's the noisiest sound
Keep your ear to the ground
Just listen

It's two friends playing snap
It's your hands when you clap
"Please beware – mind the gap!"
Just listen

It's the beat of your heart
It's a skill, it's an art
Do you want to be smart?
Then shhhhhhhhhhhhhhh...

Just listen

Adam's Apples

(A poem brought to you by the letter A)

Adam ate apples
Adam ate ALL apples
Admired and adored apples
Annie's apples
Akira's apples
Aaron's apples
Amir's apples
Adam ate ANY apples

Adam avoided almonds
Avocados
Aubergines
Anchovies
Ackee
Asparagus
And also antelope
As Adam ate apples

Appetizing apple advertisements attracted Adam
Adam ate apples abundantly
Adam ate apples avariciously
Affirming "Apples are astonishing!
Apples are astounding!

Apples are awesome!"
Adam assembled apples
Adam amassed apples
Adam absorbed apples
Adam ALWAYS ate apples

Abruptly
Adam's abdomen ached acutely
"AAAAAAAAAAAARGH!"
Absolute agony!
Adam 'ad acquired an apple allergy
An awful, appalling, atrocious apple allergy
AMBULANCE!
AMBULANCE!
AMBULANCE!
(Amazingly an ambulance arrived automatically)

Afterwards
Adults advised Adam
"Avert additional anxiety and accidents
Abandon apples!"
Adam acted accordingly

Avowing absolute apple abstinence
And apprehensively announcing an appropriate
amendment

Adam ate apricots
Adam ate ALL apricots
Admired and adored apricots
Annie's apricots
Akira's apricots
Aaron's apricots
Amir's apricots
Adam ate ANY apricots...

You Say...

You say happy
I say delighted
You say eager
I say excited

You say handy
I say practical
You say clever
I say tactical

You say pretty
I say beautiful
You say loyal
I say dutiful

You say stupid
I say risible
You say in view
I say visible

You say solid
I say non-porous
Since I borrowed
Your new thesaurus

Beware of the Dog!

Beware of the Dog!
He's fixed his eyes on you
Beware of the Dog!
He practises Kung Fu

Beware of the Dog!
He packs a powerful punch
Beware of the Dog!
He's yet to eat his lunch

Beware of the Dog!
He's such a serious threat
Beware of the Dog!
Ask the bite-scarred vet

Beware of the Dog!
He's incredibly large
Beware of the Dog!
He's so supercharged

Beware of the Dog!
He devoured the postman
Beware of the Dog!
Or you'll be doggie toast man

Beware of the Dog!
He does dangerous stuff
Beware of the Dog!

SNARRRRRRL!

WOOF! WOOF! WOOF!
GGGGGGROWL!

RUFF! RUFF! RUFF!

Lap Cat

She curls up
She furls up
She snuggles and swirls up
Enjoying an afternoon nap

So furry
So purry
So cinnamon whirly
My fine feline friend on my lap

Verbing

Hope is hoping
Rob is robbing
Flo is flowing
Bob is bobbing

Dawn is dawning
Josh is joshing
Wade is wading
Floss is flossing

Pat is patting
Harry is harrying
Nick is nicking
Carrie is carrying

Mark is marking
Sue is suing
Blossom is blossoming

But what are YOU doing?

Blank

It could become a great story book
or the simplest aeroplane,
the most mind-boggling maths equation,
a long colourful paper chain.

It might turn into a self-portrait
or a birthday card for a friend,
an origami brontosaurus,
a letter for someone to send.

The script for a fab fantastic film
or a poem that lasts an age.
Who knows what magic's awaiting us
when presented with a blank page?

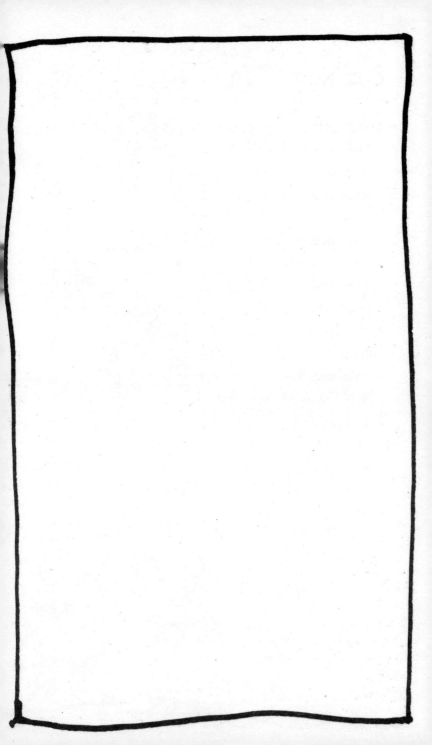

R a ndo m

Spaghetti
Confetti
Piano
Your settee
It's completely ran
Dom

Wise wizard
Pet lizard
Pork Sausage
My gizzard
It's definitely
r **An** **d** o M

Half-burnt toast
High lamp post
Botswana
A dead ghost
It's absolutely
R
    AN
D
o
    M

Fake flippers
Fried kippers
A, B, C, D, E, F, G, H, I, J, K, L, M, N, Z, O, P,
Q, R, S, T, U, V, W, X, Y, Y
Nail clippers
It's totally modnar

La la la la la la BOING!
Chandelier
$x = 2y - 7$
Squabble
It's obviously
Ra nd oM

Hot chilli
Caerphilly
X factor
So silly
It's unmistakably
amdorn
Rrrrrrrrrrrrrr a n d o m
<u>RANDOM!</u>

(PS Hiccup, tinkle, pufferfish)

Metaphor Man

He eats villains for lunch
When it comes to the crunch
Who's the pick of the bunch?
It's Metaphor Man

If your blue sky turns grey
He'll just blow it away
Who's that saving the day?
It's Metaphor Man

A dependable rock
Bound to come out on top
Who's the cream of the crop?
It's Metaphor Man

Stops bad guys in their tracks
Watching everyone's back
Who's the ace in the pack?
It's Metaphor Man

Who is truth?
Who is light?
Who is speed?
Who is might?
BOOM!
Who is live dynamite?
It's Metaphor Man

TEMPER

I lost my TEMPER
I watched it go
Where it ran off to
I'll never know

I lost my TEMPER
With one LOUD SHOUT
Opened my mouth wide
Saw it JUMP out

I lost my TEMPER
BOOM! BOOM! BOOM! BOOM!
Heard the EXPLOSIONS
All round the room

I lost my TEMPER
When I got MAD
Had many TANTRUMS
But this was BAD

I lost my TEMPER
Waved it goodbye
Now I'm so sorry
I made you cry

Places

If it's true that people
Tie knots in Nottingham
Drive cars in Cardiff
Make glass in Glasgow
Ring bells in Belfast
Do less in Leicester
Drink water in Waterloo
Burn things in Burnley
Keep wolves in Wolverhampton,
　　swans in Swansea,
　　and eels in Ealing
Crawl in Crawley
Fall down in Falkirk
Bark in Barking (surely not?)
Read in Reading
Are born in Bournemouth
But live in Liverpool

Then what do they do in Llanfairpwllgwyngyllgo
　　gerychwyrndrobwllllantysiliogogogoch?*

*This is a real village in Wales

The Rougher, Tougher Pufferfish

I'm the rougher, tougher pufferfish,
pick on me if you dare.
Much meaner than most other fish,
please handle me with care.

Inflating like a spiky sphere
when threatened with attack,
I'm warning you do not come near –
select another snack.

I'm the rougher, tougher pufferfish,
scourge of the Seven Seas.
Shoot poison to subdue you too
if you give me a squeeze.

My reputation is renowned.
Catch me? I wouldn't try.
You'll meet a messy end, my friend,
choose other fish to fry.

I'm the rougher, tougher pufferfish
with weapons to reveal.
So stick to sole, cod, plaice or skate
next time you want a meal.

Fright

It creeps up in the night
It's a fright
Flashes teeth that can bite
It's a fright
It hides underneath your bed
Worms its way into your head
It's a fright, fright, fright, fright, fright!

Whispers things in your ear
It's a fear
Words you don't want to hear
It's a fear
Digs down deep into your brain
It's a crashing, speeding train
It's a fear, fear, fear, fear, fear!

It could pounce anywhere
It's a scare
It's a wolf, it's a bear
It's a scare
It's a painful stomach punch
Causes you to lose your lunch
It's a scare, scare, scare, scare, scare!

It's a creak, crack or knock
It's a shock
Stops your watch and your clock
It's a shock
Warns you that the end is near
Makes this poem finish here

It's a shock, shock, shock, shock, shock!

Echo

I'm an echo, echo, echo
I rebound, bound, bound
Carbon copy, copy, copy
Of a sound, sound, sound

Making ripples, ripples, ripples
Making waves, waves, waves
Haunted houses, houses, houses
Creepy caves, caves, caves

Hitting ceilings, ceilings, ceilings
Hitting walls, walls, walls
In the distance, distance, distance
Hear me call, call, call

I'm a mimic, mimic, mimic
I'm a clone, clone, clone
Noise recurring, curring, curring
Once it's thrown, thrown, thrown

Though returning, turning, turning
I can't stay, stay, stay
I must quietly, quietly, quietly
Fade away, way, way, way, way...

Breakfast

Gesg
Gges
Segg
Ggse

Orangana
Strawapple
Pineberry
Melofruit

Cornflakes
Cornflakes
Cornflakes
Cornflakes (to be continued...)

£££££
$$$$$
~~¥¥¥¥¥~~

T⋆

(⋆Or, if you're rushing to get to school or work:
scrambled eggs, mixed fruit, cereal, bread, tea)

Living Next Door to a Viking

He stands with a spear in his doorway
From Sweden or Denmark or Norway
Iron helmet and beard
It's just as I feared
I'm living next door to a Viking

He tells me he travels by longboat
Wears animal hide and a fur coat
His favourite drink
Is strong mead, I think
I'm living next door to a Viking

We welcomed him then he betrayed us
Insisting he's set to invade us
Since he first appeared
Things have got quite weird
I'm living next door to a Viking

He's shining his shields every Sunday
And sharpening swords every Monday
A huge fan of Thor
And weapons and war
I'm living next door to a Viking

An expert on our Middle Ages
Throws tempers and tantrums and rages
Valhalla's his aim
He's fighting again!
I'm living next door to a Viking

Surprise Package

Cara, Cassie
Georgia, Gemma
Rosie, Roxy
Erin, Emma
What will we call Mum's new baby?

Amy, Ali
Uma, Una
Bella, Becky
Lauren, Luna
What will we call Mum's new baby?

Lizzy, Lara
Sue, Serena
Mandy, Megan
Ann, Alina
What will we call Mum's new baby?

Abi, Alice
Heidi, Hannah
Tegan, Tara
Jess, Joanna
What will we call Mum's new baby?

Dannielle, Debbi
Precious, Polly
Zena, Zahra
Maisie, Molly
What will we call Mum's new baby?
What will we call Mum's new baby?
WHAT WILL WE CALL MUM'S NEW
BABY?*

*When she finally arrived, we decided to call HIM Max!

The Day I Ate My School

Please, Sir, I'm truly sorry,
I know I broke the rules,
but I felt so hungry lunchtime
I ate the entire school.

Consuming every classroom,
the field and playground too,
the fences and the front gate,
the library and the loos.

I swallowed up the staffroom,
the teachers sat within,
the office swiftly followed
by every litter bin.

The children were delicious,
the TAs great to snack.
Computers, sports equipment
fed my hunger pang attack.

The roof and walls were yummy,
the doors and halls divine,
the cars and carpark such a treat,
all washed down with some wine.

The Head yelled, "Stop! Detention!
After the home time bell!"
I turned around with open mouth,
devouring her as well.

Now as you are reading this
you've no need to be sad,
as that was definitely the best school dinner
that I've ever had.

(*Mmmmmmm! Burp!*)

Rucksack

My rucksack resembles a bottomless sack
Jam-packed with my stuff, always stuck to my back

Containing a book and two comics for reading
An apple, a sandwich on which I'll be feeding
A bottle of sparkling water for drinking
My parents suggest it's got our kitchen sink in

It carries a pencil, blank paper, fun stickers
A padlock, an odd sock, a spare pair of knickers
A wad of clean tissues, a big bar of chocolate
My door keys and phone tightly zipped in the
　　pocket

I've squeezed in my tablet, along with my glasses
Although I'm unsure as to where my bus pass is
My baseball cap languishes down at the bottom
With trinkets and items I've long since forgotten

90

It holds a small stash of emergency money
Along with some sun cream in case it's too sunny
You'll find an umbrella for days when it's pouring
I'm sure if I tried I could still fit lots more in

My rucksack resembles a bottomless sack
Jam-packed with my stuff, always stuck to my back

Favourite Words

Onomatopoeia, banana
Streeeeeeeetch, flip-flop
Discombobulated, zinnidious*
Fungi, platypus, plop

Kalamazoo, Timbuktu
Croissant**, corrugated
Pandemonium, sphinx
Fizz (extremely underrated)

Shenanigans, nebulae
Cellophane, schmooze
Codswallop, cacophony...

Which words would YOU choose?

I made that one up
**Only with a strong French accent*

The Last Poem

The last poem in this book,
I never stand a chance.
While other odes are favourites
I'm just a passing glance.
Most people move real rapidly
through pages 1, 2, 3...
but by the time they reach the back
they're far too tired for me.

The last poem in this book,
the one to close the show.
Though I asked to be somewhere else
there was nowhere to go.
Now I am every bit as good
as any of the rest.
My idea's fresh, my rhymes are fun,
in fact I think I'm best!

The last poem in this book,
the end, the final word.
Deep down I'm devastated
over all that has occurred.
So if you want to cheer me up
and free me from this curse,
when reading this collection next…

please, please turn to me first!

About the Poet and the Illustrator

NEAL ZETTER began writing poetry when he was six years old. Since 1994 he has staged his fun poetry-writing workshops and performances in hundreds of schools and libraries in the UK and beyond, teaching 3-103 year olds to create their own fantastic poetry.

He has won the Silver Book Award, been acclaimed by the Reading Agency and Book Trust, had poems on London's buses, in the Guardian newspaper and in many anthologies. He has performed his adult poems on radio, in the Royal Festival Hall, at a League 2 football match, festivals, weddings and funerals (really), countless top West End Comedy clubs and hosted his own club for ten years. This is Neal's 12th book, his second for Otter-Barry Books, following *The Universal Zoo*. For all things Neal see **cccpworkshops.co.uk**

WILL HUGHES is an illustrator of children books from Malvern in Worcestershire. He always enjoyed drawing pictures and creating stories, so studied at Hereford College of Arts and then for a degree in illustration at the University of Edinburgh. He mainly works in ink and watercolour because he likes how that lends itself to quick and lively illustrations with hopefully some character and humour. In 2019 Will was part of the Picturehooks Mentoring Scheme, which culminated in two pieces of his work being exhibited at the Scottish National Gallery of Modern Art. He has illustrated six published books including *The Universal Zoo*, also written by Neal Zetter and published by Otter-Barry books, and he enjoys running workshops for children about drawing and thinking of stories.